SUPERCROSS MOTORCYCLES

by Lisa Bullard

Lerner Publications Company • Minneapolis

This book is for Nadine: friend for life, super-cross my heart.

Lerner Publications Company
A division of Lerner Publishing Group
241 First Avenue North
Minneapolis, MN 55401

Website address: www.lernerbooks.com

Words in **bold** type are explained in a glossary on page 30.

Library of Congress Cataloging-in-Publication Data

Bullard, Lisa.
    Supercross motorcycles / by Lisa Bullard.
      p.   cm. — (Pull ahead books)
    Includes index.
    ISBN-13: 978-0-8225-6010-4 (lib. bdg. : alk. paper)
    ISBN-10: 0-8225-6010-0 (lib. bdg. : alk. paper)
    1. Trail bikes—Juvenile literature. 2. Supercross—Juvenile
literature. I. Title. II. Series.
    TL441.B85 2007
    629.227'5—dc22   2005022020

Manufactured in the United States of America
1 2 3 4 5 6 — JR — 12 11 10 09 08 07

Have you ever seen a flying
motorcycle?

Supercross motorcycles don't fly.
But they sure can jump! They are built
to handle bumps and jumps.

They are also built to race.

Supercross races are held in big sports stadiums. People must build the track before the race.

They use bulldozers to shape big piles
of dirt. The finished track is full of
jumps, bumps, and turns.

Riders must go around the track many times during a race. Each trip around the track is called a **lap**.

This supercross rider is getting ready to race. Riders wear lots of gear. The gear protects them during a crash.

A helmet protects the rider's head.

The race is about to begin! The riders line up at the gate.

The gate drops. And the race is on!

The motorcycles roar around the track.
The riders fight for the lead.

Supercross
riders must
do more than
race fast.
They must
handle jumps
and turns.

14

The rider stands on **foot pegs** for much of the race.

The rider leans into the turn. He sticks out a foot to stay balanced.

Big jumps send the motorcycles high into the air.

Parts of the track have rows of bumps called **whoops.** The motorcycles bounce up and down on the whoops.

The
motorcycle
has springs.
They help
make bumpy
landings a
little softer.

An **engine** powers the motorcycle.
It is set high on the motorcycle.
This keeps the engine from hitting
the ground.

The **throttle** is on the handlebars.
The throttle controls the engine. The
rider twists the throttle to go faster.

The rider
squeezes
the front
brake lever
to slow
down.

Supercross motorcycles have
knobby tires. The knobs help the
tires hold onto the dirt track.

Oh no! This motorcycle has crashed!
Is the rider okay?

Yes! He is just fine! He'll pick up his motorcycle and keep racing.

These riders are still going strong.
They race for the finish line. The first
to cross will be the winner!

This winner is showing off his skills. He is doing a stunt at the **finish line jump.**

Facts about Supercross Motorcycles

- Supercross is a lot like motocross racing. But motocross races are held outdoors on long dirt tracks. The tracks are so long that fans cannot see the whole track at the same time. People invented supercross so fans could see all of the action from their seats in a stadium.

- Motocross tracks are longer than supercross tracks. But the jumps on a supercross track are usually bigger.

- Supercross racers sometimes jump as high as three stories into the air.

- People sometimes use a shorter name for supercross. They call it SX.

Parts of a Supercross Motorcycle

throttle brake lever

engine

foot peg

knobby tires

Glossary

brake lever: a handle that the rider pulls to slow down a motorcycle

engine: the part that powers a motorcycle. Most motorcycle engines run on gas.

finish line jump: a jump at the end of the race

foot pegs: low posts on each side of the motorcycle where riders can stand

knobby tires: tires with rubber knobs, or bumps, that help grip the track

lap: one full trip around a track

throttle: the part that controls the engine and makes the motorcycle go faster

whoops: a row of bumps on a supercross track

More about Supercross motorcycles

Check out these books and this website to find out more about Supercross motorcycles.

Books

Armentrout, David and Patricia. *Dirt Bikes.* Vero Beach, FL: Rourke Publishing, 2006.
This book has lots of text and pictures about the kind of off-road motorcycle that race in Supercross.

Budd, E. S. *Off-Road Motorcycles.* Chanhassen, MN: The Child's World, 2004.
This book includes many different kinds of off-road motorcycles.

Hill, Lee Sullivan. *Motorcycles.* Minneapolis: Lerner Publications Company, 2004.
Learn about many different kinds of motorcycles from this fun book.

Website

American Motorcycle Association: Just for Kids!
http://www.amadirectlink.com/kids/
This page on the American Motorcycle Association website has drawings of racing motorcycles that can be printed out and colored.

Index

Photo Acknowledgments

The photographs in this book are used with permission of: © Steve Bruhn, pp. 3, 4, 6, 7, 9, 10, 14, 16, 18, 19, 20, 22, 23, 24, 25, 26; © Jeff Kardas/Getty Images, p. 5; © Franck Faugere/DPPI/Icon SMI, p. 8; © Troy Wayrynen/NewSport/CORBIS, p. 11; © Albert Gea/Reuters/CORBIS, p. 12; © Tim Tadder/NewSport/CORBIS, pp. 13, 15, 17, 21, 27.

Cover photo used with permission of © Tim Tadder/NewSport/CORBIS.